A
MONTH
of PRAYER
WITH ST. JOHN OF THE CROSS

A
MONTH
of PRAYER

WITH ST. JOHN OF THE CROSS

Wyatt North
BOOKS THAT INSPIRE

INTRODUCTION

Saint John of the Cross (1542-1591) was a major reformer of the Carmelite Order. He was canonized as a saint by Pope Benedict XIII in 1726. What he accomplished in the monasteries paralleled what Saint Theresa of Avila did in the convents. Together, these two saints are considered the founders of the Discalced Carmelites. In fact, the two saints were friends and corresponded regularly.

St. John of the Cross was given such a name on account of the centrality the cross played in his path toward spiritual illumination. He is widely known for his poetry and reflections on what he termed the "dark night of the soul," a period of struggle and turmoil against the flesh that he believed all who seek spiritual enlightenment must endure on the path to experiencing illumination by the Holy Spirit.

In these meditations, we will consider St. John of the Cross's three most well-known works: *Dark Night of the Soul, Ascent of Mount Carmel,* and *The Spiritual Canticle.* These are not, however, disjointed reflections that can be read in any order. What has been assembled here is an introduction to the entire path that St. John of the Cross laid out as a method of spiritual progress.

DAY 1

In today's meditation, St. John of the Cross reminds us how, after a time of being nurtured as a mother does a new infant, those who progress in the faith are often set upon challenges. The child must learn to walk. In the process, the child might stumble and bruise a knee or elbow. So, too, for those who progress in the faith, after a time, we are no longer nursed and nurtured but set to labor in the things of God, tested with trials and doubts, not that we might fall but that we might learn to walk and even run into God's arms more fervently.

Meditations from St. John of the Cross

It must be known, then, that the soul, after it has been definitely converted to the service of God, is, as a rule, spiritually nurtured and caressed by God, even as is the tender child by its loving mother, who warms it with the heat of her bosom and nurtures it with sweet milk and soft and pleasant food, and carries it and caresses it in her arms; but, as the child grows bigger, the mother gradually ceases caressing it, and, hiding her tender love, puts bitter aloes upon her sweet breast, sets down the child from her arms and makes it walk upon its feet, so that it may lose the habits of a child and betake itself to more important and substantial occupations. The loving mother is like the grace of God, for, as soon as the soul is regenerated by its new warmth and fervour for the service of God, He treats it in the same way; He makes it to find spiritual milk, sweet and delectable, in all

1

the things of God, without any labour of its own, and also great pleasure in spiritual exercises, for here God is giving to it the breast of His tender love, even as to a tender.

St. John of the Cross.
Dark Night of the Soul

Additional Biblical Reflections: 1 Corinthians 3:1-3; 1 Peter 2:1-25; Hebrews 5:11-14.

Prayer

Lord, now that we have been nurtured like babes on your sweet milk, we are tasked to begin taking steps through the challenges of life. Guide us through the "dark night" of the soul as we learn to rely on you, to trust your direction, and follow your voice even as we wander through the wilderness of the world. Amen.

DAY 2

One of the most common temptations that befall the young of faith is that when eager to perform acts of piety and good works, pride quickly wells up, and one begins to think they have become something godly. Here, St. John of the Cross reminds us about the trapping of the Pharisee, who believed he was greater than other men. Instead, as we grow in the faith, we must come to see ourselves evermore in contrast to the glories of God, whom we come to know more intimately. The more we know God, the more we should see, by comparison, that we are flawed and broken creatures dependent on His grace and mercy.

Meditations from St. John of the Cross

As these beginners feel themselves to be very fervent and diligent in spiritual things and devout exercises, from this prosperity (although it is true that holy things of their own nature cause humility) there often comes to them, through their imperfections, a certain kind of secret pride, whence they come to have some degree of satisfaction with their works and with themselves. And hence there comes to them likewise a certain desire, which is somewhat vain, and at times very vain, to speak of spiritual things in the presence of others, and sometimes even to teach such things rather than to learn them. They condemn others in their heart when they see that they have not the kind of devotion which they themselves desire; and sometimes they even say this in words, herein resembling the Pharisee, who boasted of himself, praising God for his own good works and despising the publican.

In these persons the devil often increases the fervour that they have and the desire to perform these and other works more frequently, so that their pride and presumption may grow greater. For the devil knows quite well that all these works and virtues which they perform are not only valueless to them, but even become vices in them. And such a degree of evil are some of these persons wont to reach that they would have none appear good save themselves; and thus, in deed and word, whenever the opportunity occurs, they condemn them and slander them, beholding the mote in their brother's eye and not considering the beam which is in their own; they strain at another's gnat and themselves swallow a camel.

St. John of the Cross.
The Dark Night of the Soul.

Additional Biblical Reflections: Proverbs 16:18; Luke 18:11ff.; James 4:6

Prayer

Dearest Lord, as we draw nearer to you, let us always see that by comparison to your glory, we are but humble creatures, dependent on your every grace. Grant this: that pride might not set us on a course in the opposite direction from which we were first set when you granted us your Spirit. Amen.

DAY 3

I t is easy to be distracted by all the *methods* of achieving piety and lose focus on the heart of the matter, which is, quite literally, the devotion of the *heart* itself. How quickly—although starting on the path toward piety with the right intentions—do we fail to see the results we seek and end up jumping from practice to practice as if it is the external thing that must change rather than the condition of our hearts. In today's mediation, St. John of the Cross warns of such ritualism—vain repetitions devoid of the heart's devotion.

Meditations from St. John of the Cross

Many of these beginners have also at times great spiritual avarice. They will be found to be discontented with the spirituality which God gives them; and they are very disconsolate and querulous because they find not in spiritual things the consolation that they would desire. Many can never have enough of listening to counsels and learning spiritual precepts, and of possessing and reading many books which treat of this matter, and they spend their time on all these things rather than on works of mortification and the perfecting of the inward poverty of spirit which should be theirs. Furthermore, they burden themselves with images and rosaries which are very curious; now they put down one, now take up another; now they change about, now change back again; now they want this kind of thing, now that, preferring one kind of cross to another, because it is more curious.

And others you will see adorned with agnus deis and relics and tokens, like children with trinkets. Here I condemn the attachment of the heart, and the affection which they have for the nature, multitude and curiosity of these things, inasmuch as it is quite contrary to poverty of spirit which considers only the substance of devotion, makes use only of what suffices for that end and grows weary of this other kind of multiplicity and curiosity. For true devotion must issue from the heart, and consist in the truth and substances alone of what is represented by spiritual things; all the rest is affection and attachment proceeding from imperfection; and in order that one may pass to any kind of perfection it is necessary for such desires to be killed.

St. John of the Cross.
A Life. Chapter 19

Additional Biblical Reflections: Proverbs 14:12-15; Matthew 6:7; Mark 7:3-9.

Prayer

Lord, you have blessed us with many means and methods whereby we might draw closer to you. Let us not forget the ends of our piety for the sake of the means. Guide us ever by your presence so that we might engage in true piety with the devotion of our hearts and not satisfy our vanities. Amen.

DAY 4

It is easy to assume that amid pious acts, attending mass, saying our prayers, or even receiving the Eucharist, we are immune from spiritual weakness or diabolical assault. This is because we are vulnerable during such moments, so human flesh, the Devil and his demons, or even fear, can lead us astray. This is a part of the "dark night" of the soul that St. John of the Cross describes—a period of growth in the faith where it sometimes seems that no matter what we do, the Lord is absent, and we are left alone, wandering as spiritual beggars.

Meditations from St. John of the Cross

Many of these beginners have many other imperfections than those which I am describing with respect to each of the deadly sins, but these I set aside, in order to avoid prolixity, touching upon a few of the most important, which are, as it were, the origin and cause of the rest. And thus, with respect to this sin of luxury (leaving apart the falling of spiritual persons into this sin, since my intent is to treat of the imperfections which have to be purged by the dark night), they have many imperfections which might be described as spiritual luxury, not because they are so, but because the imperfections proceed from spiritual things. For it often comes to pass that, in their very spiritual exercises, when they are powerless to prevent it, there arise and assert themselves in the sensual part of the soul impure acts and motions, and sometimes this happens even when the spirit is deep in prayer, or engaged in the Sacrament of Penance or in the Eucharist. These things are not, as I say, in their power; they proceed from one of three causes.

The first cause from which they often proceed is the pleasure which human nature takes in spiritual things. For when the spirit and the sense are pleased, every part of a man is moved by that pleasure to delight according to its proportion and nature. For then the spirit, which is the higher part, is moved to pleasure and delight in God; and the sensual nature, which is the lower part, is moved to pleasure and delight of the senses, because it cannot possess and lay hold upon aught else, and it therefore lays hold upon that which comes nearest to itself, which is the impure and sensual...

The second cause whence these rebellions sometimes proceed is the devil, who, in order to disquiet and disturb the soul, at times when it is at prayer or is striving to pray, contrives to stir up these motions of impurity in its nature; and if the soul gives heed to any of these, they cause it great harm. For through fear of these not only do persons become lax in prayer—which is the aim of the devil when he begins to strive with them—but some give up prayer altogether, because they think that these things attack them more during that exercise than apart from it, which is true, since the devil attacks them then more than at other times, so that they may give up spiritual exercises...

The third source whence these impure motions are apt to proceed in order to make war upon the soul is often the fear which such persons have conceived for these impure representations and motions. Something that they see or say or think brings them to their mind, and this makes them afraid, so that they suffer from them through no fault of their own.

St. John of the Cross.
Dark Night of the Soul

Additional Biblical Reflections: Matthew 26:24; Mark 14:38; Ephesians 6:7.

Prayer

Dear Lord, guard our hearts and make us ever mindful that the flesh and the Devil, even our fear, is always working against our desire to know you more. Sustain us through your presence, especially when we are in prayer and engaged in spiritual disciplines so that through them, we might be led more closely toward you. Amen.

DAY 5

The Catechism describes the sin of wrath as the taking out of one's anger on an innocent person, or at least, unworthy of the degree of "wrath" we levy against them. According to St. John of the Cross, this is one of the temptations that beginners in spiritual paths are most vulnerable to. This often stems from the fact that early in our spiritual development, the feelings that we mistake for spiritual progress are often fleeting. When our emotions wane, we often think we have lost our contact with the divine and that our progress has been for naught. Then, out of desperation, we often fall prey to the sin of wrath.

Meditations from St. John of the Cross

By reason of the concupiscence which many beginners have for spiritual consolations, their experience of these consolations is very commonly accompanied by many imperfections proceeding from the sin of wrath; for, when their delight and pleasure in spiritual things come to an end, they naturally become embittered, and bear that lack of sweetness which they have to suffer with a bad grace, which affects all that they do; and they very easily become irritated over the smallest matter—sometimes, indeed, none can tolerate them. This frequently happens after they have been very pleasantly recollected in prayer according to sense; when their pleasure and delight therein come to an end, their nature is naturally vexed and disappointed, just as is the child when they take it from the breast of which it was enjoying the sweetness. There is no sin in this natural vexation, when it is not permitted to indulge itself, but only imperfection, which must be purged by the aridity and severity of the dark night.

There are other of these spiritual persons, again, who fall into another kind of spiritual wrath: this happens when they become irritated at the sins of others, and keep watch on those others with a sort of uneasy zeal. At times the impulse comes to them to reprove them angrily, and occasionally they go so far as to indulge it and set themselves up as masters of virtue. All this is contrary to spiritual meekness.

St. John of the Cross.
Dark Night of the Soul

Additional Biblical Reflections: Psalm 37:8; Proverbs 14:29; Ephesians 4:26.

Prayer

Lord, you are a God of mercy and grace. Yet we often turn easily to anger and wrath. Grant us your peace and make us ever aware of our anger so that it does not turn into wrath. Lead us, instead, to your mercies so that we might remain grateful rather than angry, even when the emotions of our faith wane. In Jesus's name. Amen.

DAY 6

To this point, most of St. John of the Cross's meditations have not been entirely encouraging. He insists the spiritual life must go through a "dark night of the soul," a period where we see all that we lack so that we might gratefully receive the gifts the Lord wishes us to have. It is during this "dark night," the time when it *feels* that God is far away, that He is actually drawing near and doing some of His most important work on our spirits through His Spirit.

Meditations from St. John of the Cross

This is the first and principal benefit caused by this arid and dark night of contemplation: the knowledge of oneself and of one's misery. For, besides the fact that all the favours which God grants to the soul are habitually granted to them enwrapped in this knowledge, these aridities and this emptiness of the faculties, compared with the abundance which the soul experienced aforetime and the difficulty which it finds in good works, make it recognize its own lowliness and misery, which in the time of its prosperity it was unable to see... In the first place, the soul learns to commune with God with more respect and more courtesy, such as a soul must ever observe in converse with the Most High. These it knew not in its prosperous times of comfort and consolation, for that comforting favour which it experienced made its craving for God somewhat bolder than was fitting, and discourteous and ill-considered... And here we must note another excellent benefit which there is in this night and aridity of the desire of sense, since we have had occasion to speak of it. It is that, in this dark night of the desire (to the end that the words of the Prophet may be fulfilled, namely: 'Thy light shall shine in the darkness'), God will enlighten the soul, giving it knowledge, not only of its lowliness and wretchedness, as we have said, but likewise of the greatness and excellence of God... Let it suffice here to have described these imperfections, among the many to be found in the lives of those that are in this first state of beginners, so that it may be seen how greatly they need God to set them in the state of proficients. This He does by bringing them into the dark night whereof we now speak; wherein He weans them from the breasts of these sweetnesses and pleasures, gives them pure aridities and inward darkness, takes from them all these irrelevances and puerilities, and by very different means causes them to win the virtues. For, however assiduously the beginner practises the mortification in himself of all these actions and passions of his, he can never completely succeed—very far from it—until God shall work it in him passively by means of the purgation of the said night. Of this I would fain speak in some way that may be profitable; may God, then, be pleased to give me His Divine light, because this is very needful in a night that is so dark and a matter that is so difficult to describe and to expound.

St. John of the Cross, *T
he Dark Night of the Soul*

Additional Biblical Reflections: Exodus 33:3; Isiah 53:10; Psalm 38:3.

Prayer

Dearest Lord, while we go through many trials, temptations, and tribulations in this world, you are always at work through it all. Lead us to see your light as it penetrates the darkness of our lives so that we might endure through the shadowy sufferings of this life and persist into life everlasting. Amen.

DAY 7

For St. John of the Cross, spiritual progress is not linear. One does not pass through the dark night, find the light, and never experience spiritual darkness again. Rather, as one progresses, it is more a cyclical pattern whereby one gains spiritual insight through darkness, enjoys God's good things, and then might be subject to darkness again in a season when the flesh again exerts itself. But every time one passes through this darkness, God uses it to bring one through to the light with new insight, greater awareness of God's ways, and growth toward better holiness.

Meditations from St. John of the Cross

This night, which, as we say, is contemplation, produces in spiritual persons two kinds of darkness or purgation, corresponding to the two parts of man's nature—namely, the sensual and the spiritual. And thus the one night or purgation will be sensual, wherein the soul is purged according to sense, which is subdued to the spirit; and the other is a night or purgation which is spiritual, wherein the soul is purged and stripped according to the spirit, and subdued and made ready for the union of love with God. The night of sense is common and comes to many: these are the beginners; and of this night we shall speak first. The night of the spirit is the portion of very few, and these are they that are already practised and proficient, of whom we shall treat hereafter. The first purgation or night is bitter and terrible to sense, as we shall now show. *The second bears no comparison with it, for it is horrible and awful to the spirit, as we shall show presently. Since the night of sense is first in order and comes first, we shall first of all say something about it briefly, since more is written of it, as of a thing that is more common; and we shall pass on to treat more fully of the spiritual night, since very little has been said of this, either in speech or in writing, and very little is known of it, even by experience. Since, then, the conduct of these beginners upon the way of God is ignoble, and has much to do with their love of self and their own inclinations, as has been explained above, God desires to lead them farther. He seeks to bring them out of that ignoble kind of love to a higher degree of love for Him, to free them from the ignoble exercises of sense and meditation (wherewith, as we have said, they go seeking God so unworthily and in so many ways that are unbefitting), and to lead them to a kind of spiritual exercise wherein they can commune with Him more abundantly and are freed more completely from imperfections. For they have now had practice for some time in the way of virtue and have persevered in meditation and prayer, whereby, through the sweetness and pleasure that they have found therein, they have lost their love of the things of the world and have gained some degree of spiritual strength in God; this has enabled them to some extent to refrain from creature desires, so that for God's sake they are now able to suffer a light burden and a little aridity without turning back to a time which they found more pleasant. When they are going about these spiritual exercises with the greatest delight and pleasure, and when they believe that the sun of Divine favour is shining most brightly upon them, God turns all this light of theirs into darkness, and shuts against them the door and the source of the sweet spiritual water which they were tasting in God whensoever and for as long as they desired…For, as I have said, God now sees that they have grown a little, and are becoming strong enough to lay aside their swaddling clothes and be taken from the gentle breast; so He sets them down from His arms and teaches them to walk on their own feet; which they feel to be very strange, for everything seems to be going wrong with them.*

St. John of the Cross,
The Dark Night of the Soul

Additional Biblical Reflections: Romans 5:3-5; John 16:33; James 1:2-4.

Prayer

Lord, let us never imagine in this life that we have arrived at spiritual perfection. For the moment we think we have achieved it, our pride and other various sins arise from the flesh to remind us that we have not, in fact, achieved perfect godliness. Let us embrace the darkness and the light alike, knowing that you are in all and work through all to bring us closer to you. Amen.

DAY 8

Today, St. John of the Cross offers practical advice for when we are going through the dark night of the soul. At such moments, we may feel restless, with the need to do *something* to lift ourselves out of the discomfort of our condition. However, in such moments, becoming a busybody is often counterproductive. Instead, St. John of the Cross recommends that we simply find time to do *nothing*. We should find moments of peace and quiet—when we do not focus on any particular object or meditation but simply allow ourselves to exist in the knowledge that God is present, not because of the discomfort of the dark night, but, in many ways, because of it.

Meditations from St. John of the Cross

During the time, then, of the aridities of this night of sense (wherein God effects the change of which we have spoken above, drawing forth the soul from the life of sense into that of the spirit—that is, from meditation to contemplation—wherein it no longer has any power to work or to reason with its faculties concerning the things of God, as has been said), spiritual persons suffer great trials, by reason not so much of the aridities which they suffer, as of the fear which they have of being lost on the road, thinking that all spiritual blessing is over for them and that God has abandoned them since they find no help or pleasure in good things. Then they grow weary, and endeavour (as they have been accustomed to do) to concentrate their faculties with some degree of pleasure upon some object of meditation, thinking that, when they are not doing this and yet are conscious of making an effort, they are doing nothing. This effort they make not without great inward repugnance and unwillingness on the part of their soul, which was taking pleasure in being in that quietness and ease, instead of working with its faculties. So they have abandoned the one pursuit, yet draw no profit from the other; for, by seeking what is prompted by their own spirit, they lose the spirit of tranquillity and peace which they had before. And thus they are like to one who abandons what he has done in order to do it over again, or to one who leaves a city only to re-enter it, or to one who is hunting and lets his prey go in order to hunt it once more. This is useless here, for the soul will gain nothing further by conducting itself in this way, as has been said... t is well for those who find themselves in this condition to take comfort, to persevere in patience and to be in no wise afflicted. Let them trust in God, Who abandons not those that seek Him with a simple and right heart, and will not fail to give them what is needful for the road, until He bring them into the clear and pure light of love. This last He will give them by means of that other dark night, that of the spirit, if they merit His bringing them thereto.

The way in which they are to conduct themselves in this night of sense is to devote themselves not at all to reasoning and meditation, since this is not the time for it, but to allow the soul to remain in peace and quietness, although it may seem clear to them that they are doing nothing and are wasting their time, and although it may appear to them that it is because of their weakness that they have no desire in that state to think of anything. The truth is that they will be doing quite sufficient if they have patience and persevere in prayer without making any effort.

St. John of the Cross.

The Dark Night of the Soul

Additional Biblical Reflections: 1 Kings 19:11-13; Psalm 46:10; 2 Corinthians 6:4-8.

Prayer

Lord, you often come to us in the stillness. During your earthly pilgrimage, you, too, took moments to depart from the business of the world to simply commune with the Father in quiet. Quell our restlessness, particularly during seasons of the dark night in the soul, so we might hear your voice, which will lead us through every condition of this life. Amen.

DAY 9

There is no shame in recognizing that we are spiritual children. Jesus, himself, exhorted His hearers—who thought themselves more advanced in spiritual matters than they truly were—to become *like* the little children (Matt. 18:1-5). It is quite dangerous when we are spiritual children to behave as if we are adults. Imagine a child attempting to drive a car or wield a weapon. To mature in the faith, we must embrace our childhood and take from this season of our growth what we ought to receive *as* children and allow the Spirit to give us growth in due course.

Meditations from St. John of the Cross

Therefore, since these proficients are still at a very low stage of progress, and follow their own nature closely in the intercourse and dealings which they have with God, because the gold of their spirit is not yet purified and refined, they still think of God as little children, and speak of God as little children, and feel and experience God as little children, even as Saint Paul says, because they have not reached perfection, which is the union of the soul with God. In the state of union, however, they will work great things in the spirit, even as grown men, and their works and faculties will then be Divine rather than human, as will afterwards be said. To this end God is pleased to strip them of this old man and clothe them with the new man, who is created according to God, as the Apostle says, in the newness of sense.

He strips their faculties, affections and feelings, both spiritual and sensual, both outward and inward, leaving the understanding dark, the will dry, the memory empty and the affections in the deepest affliction, bitterness and constraint, taking from the soul the pleasure and experience of spiritual blessings which it had aforetime, in order to make of this privation one of the principles which are requisite in the spirit so that there may be introduced into it and united with it the spiritual form of the spirit, which is the union of love. All this the Lord works in the soul by means of a pure and dark contemplation.

St. John of the Cross.
The Dark Night of the Soul

Additional Biblical Reflections: Matthew 18:1-5; 1 Corinthians 12:11; Ephesians 4:24.

Prayer
Dearest Lord, let us approach you as little children, eager to hear every word without any pretense that we have grown or matured more than we have, for you give us what we need in due season. Grant us such humility so that we might truly become mature disciples. Amen.

DAY 10

S t. John of the Cross does not exhort his hearers because he is more learned than other men; rather, he speaks of his own experience enduring a "dark night." Likewise, from his experience, he knows the blessings and happiness that follow. In today's meditation, we might take comfort from his example.

Meditations from St. John of the Cross

This was a great happiness and a good chance for me; for, when the faculties had been perfectly annihilated and calmed, together with the passions, desires and affections of my soul, wherewith I had experienced and tasted God after a lowly manner, I went forth from my own human dealings and operations to the operations and dealings of God. That is to say, my understanding went forth from itself, turning from the human and natural to the Divine; for, when it is united with God by means of this purgation, its understanding no longer comes through its natural light and vigour, but through the Divine Wisdom wherewith it has become united. And my will went forth from itself, becoming Divine; for, being united with Divine love, it no longer loves with its natural strength after a lowly manner, but with strength and purity from the Holy Spirit; and thus the will, which is now near to God, acts not after a human manner, and similarly the memory has become transformed into eternal apprehensions of glory. And finally, by means of this night and purgation of the old man, all the energies and affections of the soul are wholly renewed into a Divine temper and Divine delight.

St. John of the Cross,

The Dark Night of the Soul

Additional Biblical Reflections: Proverbs 3:12-18; Job 5:17-27; Philippians 4:7.

Prayer

Lord, you do not grant us a period of trial so that we might be miserable; rather, you press us through the "dark night," so we might come to know true happiness as creatures made in your image. Let us take comfort from the example of those who have gone before us, and, together with your word, trust that the path you've set us on is not one destined for misery, but one that, while suffering might befall us in the end, will result in genuine contentment. Amen.

DAY 11

According to St. John of the Cross, there are multiple nights of the soul through which one might progress in his way to spiritual perfection. In today's meditation, he bids us to consider the example of Tobias, as contained in the Book of Tobit, as he endured hardship and trial in the pursuit of his would-be wife. We hear not only the unique character of each of these three nights of the soul but the way the Lord worked through each of them to prepare Tobias for the life He had intended for him.

Meditations from St. John of the Cross

We may say that there are three reasons for which this journey made by the soul to union with God is called night. The first has to do with the point from which the soul goes forth, for it has gradually to deprive itself of desire for all the worldly things which it possessed, by denying them to itself...The second reason has to do with the mean, or the road along which the soul must travel to this union — that is, faith, which is likewise as dark as night to the understanding. The third has to do with the point to which it travels — namely, God, Who, equally, is dark night to the soul in this life. These three nights must pass through the soul — or, rather, the soul must pass through them — in order that it may come to Divine union with God.

In the book of the holy Tobias these three kinds of night were shadowed forth by the three nights which, as the angel commanded, were to pass ere the youth Tobias should be united with his bride. In the first he commanded him to burn the heart of the fish in the fire, which signifies the heart that is affectioned to, and set upon, the things of the world; which, in order that one may begin to journey toward God, must be burned and purified from all that is creature, in the fire of the love of God. And in this purgation the devil flees away, for he has power over the soul only when it is attached to things corporeal and temporal.

On the second night the angel told him that he would be admitted into the company of the holy patriarchs, who are the fathers of the faith. For, passing through the first night, which is self-privation of all objects of sense, the soul at once enters into the second night, and abides alone in faith to the exclusion, not of charity, but of other knowledge acquired by the understanding, as we shall say hereafter, which is a thing that pertains not to sense.

On the third night the angel told him that he would obtain a blessing, which is God; Who, by means of the second night, which is faith, continually communicates Himself to the soul in such a secret and intimate manner that He becomes another night to the soul, inasmuch as this said communication is far darker than those others, as we shall say presently. And, when this third night is past, which is the complete accomplishment of the communication of God in the spirit, which is ordinarily wrought in great darkness of the soul, there then follows its union with the Bride, which is the Wisdom of God. Even so the angel said likewise to Tobias that, when the third night was past, he should be united with his bride in the fear of the Lord; for, when this fear of God is perfect, love is perfect, and this comes to pass when the transformation of the soul is wrought through its love.

These three parts of the night are all one night; but, after the manner of night, it has three parts. For the first part, which is that of sense, is comparable to the beginning of night, the point at which things begin to fade from sight. And the second part, which is faith, is comparable to midnight, which is total darkness. And the third part is like the close of night, which is God, the which part is now near to the light of day. And, that we may understand this the better, we shall treat of each of these reasons separately as we proceed.

St. John of the Cross,
Ascent of Mount Carmel

Additional Biblical Reflections: Deuteronomy 31:5; Psalm 88:1; Tobit 8-14.

Prayer

Lord, all good things come from you, even our various dark nights, through which we might pass as we make spiritual progress. Guide us through each of these, as you did for your servant Tobias, so we might enjoy the blessings you have chosen to bestow upon us. Amen.

DAY 12

In today's meditation, St. John of the Cross speaks of various kinds of fasting—fasting of all the various senses (not just abstaining from food)—and the ways that we might grow through such a spiritual practice. Through various kinds of fasts, we are told, the soul comes to realize its true condition and finds instead its delights in the things of God. According to St. John of the Cross, this is necessary if we are to attain union with God.

Meditations from St. John of the Cross

Let us take an example from each of the faculties. When the soul deprives its desire of the pleasure of all that can delight the sense of hearing, the soul remains unoccupied and in darkness with respect to this faculty. And, when it deprives itself of the pleasure of all that can please the sense of sight, it remains unoccupied and in darkness with respect to this faculty also. And, when it deprives itself of the pleasure of all the sweetness of perfumes which can give it pleasure through the sense of smell, it remains equally unoccupied and in darkness according to this faculty. And, if it also denies itself the pleasure of all food that can satisfy the palate, the soul likewise remains unoccupied and in darkness. And finally, when the soul mortifies itself with respect to all the delights and pleasures that it can receive from the sense of touch, it remains, in the same way, unoccupied and in darkness with respect to this faculty. So that the soul that has denied and thrust away from itself the pleasures which come from all these things, and has mortified its desire with respect to them, may be said to be, as it were, in the darkness of night, which is naught else than an emptiness within itself of all things.

The reason for this is that, as the philosophers say, the soul, as soon as God infuses it into the body, is like a smooth, blank board upon which nothing is painted; and, save for that which it experiences through the senses, nothing is communicated to it, in the course of nature, from any other source. And thus, for as long as it is in the body, it is like one who is in a dark prison and who knows nothing, save what he is able to see through the windows of the said prison; and, if he saw nothing through them, he would see nothing in any other way. And thus the soul, save for that which is communicated to it through the senses, which are the windows of its prison, could acquire nothing, in the course of nature, in any other way.

Wherefore, if the soul rejects and denies that which it can receive through the senses, we can quite well say that it remains, as it were, in darkness and empty; since, as appears from what has been said, no light can enter it, in the course of nature, by any other means of illumination than those aforementioned.

St. John of the Cross,
Ascent of Mount Carmel

Additional Biblical Reflections: Isaiah 58:3-7; Ezra 8:21-23; Matthew 6:16-18.

Prayer

Dear Lord, you have given us all of our senses. These things are good. Yet, in the flesh, we often find ourselves blinded from spiritual matters on account of sensual delights. Grant that we might learn, through proper fasting, our true condition, and the true satisfaction that comes only through communion with you. Amen.

DAY 13

When we set our affection and attention on earthly things, are spiritual estate is limited to that upon which our hearts and minds dwell. For those whose lives are consumed by the pursuit of riches, they might become very wealthy in this life, but all they have perishes with them. St. John of the Cross evokes the example of the Israelites, who grumbled that they were hungry. The Lord provided bread from Heaven. But what if they had obsessed instead over the need to know the Lord, who'd brought them out of Egypt? Then, they might have been ready to receive the promised land, a place flowing with milk and honey, and could feast more sumptuously than they did on manna.

Meditations from St. John of the Cross

From what has been said it may be seen in some measure how great a distance there is between all that the creatures are in themselves and that which God is in Himself, and how souls that set their affections upon any of these creatures are at as great a distance as they from God; for, as we have said, love produces equality and likeness. This distance was clearly realized by Saint Augustine, who said in the Sololoquies, speaking with God: 'Miserable man that I am, when will my littleness and imperfection be able to have fellowship with Thy uprightness? Thou indeed art good, and I am evil; Thou art merciful, and I am impious; Thou art holy, I am miserable; Thou art just,

I am unjust; Thou art light, I am blind; Thou, life, I, death; Thou, medicine, I, sick; Thou, supreme truth, I, utter vanity.' All this is said by this Saint.

Wherefore, it is supreme ignorance for the soul to think that it will be able to pass to this high estate of union with God if first it void not the desire of all things, natural and supernatural, which may hinder it, according as we shall explain hereafter; for there is the greatest possible distance between these things and that which comes to pass in this estate, which is naught else than transformation in God. For this reason Our Lord, when showing us this path, said through Saint Luke: Qui non renuntiat omnibus quae possidet, non potest meus esse discipulus. This signifies: He that renounces not all things that he possesses with his will cannot be My disciple. And this is evident; for the doctrine that the Son of God came to teach was contempt for all things, whereby a man might receive as a reward the Spirit of God in himself. For, as long as the soul rejects not all things, it has no capacity to receive the Spirit of God in pure transformation... Oh, did spiritual persons but know how much good and what great abundance of spirit they lose through not seeking to raise up their desires above childish things, and how in this simple spiritual food they would find the sweetness of all things, if they desired not to taste those things! But such food gives them no pleasure, for the reason why the children of Israel received not the sweetness of all foods that was contained in the manna was that they would not reserve their desire for it alone.

St. John of the Cross,
Ascent of Mount Carmel

Additional Biblical Reflections: Exodus 34:2-3; Wisdom 16:20; Luke 14:33.

Prayer

Dear Lord, we are so easily distracted by our bodily needs, cares, concerns, and even the pleasures of this life. But you are the great giver of all good things. Let us set our hearts not on the things we seek, but on you, the great giver, so we might receive all you would give us in your abundant mercies and love. In Jesus's name. Amen.

DAY 14

In yesterday's meditation, we heard how the things that consume our passions could distract us from God's good things. Today, we hear how otherworldly matters, namely the kinds of torments and afflictions we experience in this world, can do the same. Citing several scriptures, St. John of the Cross does not minimize or dismiss such sufferings but urges us, instead, to consider God's presence and His promise as our comforter and sustainer. In such times, when the turmoil we are experiencing has become our focus, we should rather be directed to focus on the Lord.

Meditations from St. John of the Cross

The second kind of positive evil which the desires cause the soul is in their tormenting and afflicting of it, after the manner of one who is in torment through being bound with cords from which he has no relief until he be freed. And of these David says: The cords of my sins, which are my desires, have constrained me round about. And, even as one that lies naked upon thorns and briars is tormented and afflicted, even so is the soul tormented and afflicted when it rests upon its desires. For they take hold upon it and distress it and cause it pain, even as do thorns. Of these David says likewise: They compassed me about like bees, wounding me with their stings, and they were enkindled against me, like fire among thorns; for in the desires, which are the thorns, increases the fire of anguish and torment...he more intense

31

is the desire, the greater is the torment which it causes the soul. So that the torment increases with the desire; and the greater are the desires which possess the soul, the greater are its torments; for in such a soul is fulfilled, even in this life, that which is said in the Apocalypse concerning Babylon, in these words: As much as she has wished to exalt and fulfil her desires, so much give ye to her torment and anguish. And even as one that falls into the hands of his enemies is tormented and afflicted, even so is the soul tormented and afflicted that is led away by its desires… This attaining to fatness is a going forth from all pleasures of the creatures; for the creatures torment, but the Spirit of God refreshes. And thus He calls us through Saint Matthew, saying: All ye that go about tormented, afflicted and burdened with the burden of your cares and desires, go forth from them, come to Me, and I will refresh you and ye shall find for your souls the rest which your desires take from you, wherefore they are a heavy burden.

St. John of the Cross.
Ascent of Mount Carmel

Additional Biblical Reflections: Psalm 118:61; Matthew 11:28-29; Revelation 18:7.

Prayer
Your Spirit, Lord, is greater than any affliction. Let not the troubles of this world blind us from your presence. Rather, amid the most difficult seasons of life, let us fix our eyes all the more firmly upon you so that you might raise us from our misery through your promises and blessings. Amen.

DAY 15

I n today's meditation, St. John of the Cross bids us to consider our desires, which have a way of blinding us from spiritual matters. He insists that the major problem many face in their hollow pursuits of piety is they focus immediately upon trying to attain spiritual things without mortifying the flesh. This, the saint reminds us, is akin to growing a garden in a field already populated by weeds. While "weeding" the garden of our souls can be a painful and arduous process, it is necessary to experience the growth we seek.

Meditations from St. John of the Cross

The third evil that the desires cause in the soul is that they blind and darken it. Even as vapours darken the air and allow not the bright sun to shine; or as a mirror that is clouded over cannot receive within itself a clear image; or as water defiled by mud reflects not the visage of one that looks therein; even so the soul that is clouded by the desires is darkened in the understanding and allows neither the sun of natural reason nor that of the supernatural Wisdom of God to shine upon it and illumine it clearly. And thus David, speaking to this purpose, says: Mine iniquities have taken hold upon me, and I could have no power to see...Desire blinds and darkens the soul; for desire, as such, is blind, since of itself it has no understanding in itself, the reason being to it always, as it were, a child leading a blind man. And hence it comes to pass that, whensoever the soul is guided by its desire, it becomes blind; for this is as if one that sees were guided by one that sees not, which is, as it were, for both to be blind. And that which follows from this is that which Our Lord says through Saint Matthew: 'If the blind lead the blind, both fall into the pit.'… For this reason one must greatly lament the ignorance of certain men, who burden themselves with extraordinary penances and with many other voluntary practices, and think that this practice or that will suffice to bring them to the union of Divine Wisdom; but such will not be the case if they endeavour not diligently to mortify their desires. If they were careful to bestow half of that labour on this, they would profit more in a month than they profit by all the other practices in many years. For, just as it is necessary to till the earth if it is to bear fruit, and unless it be tilled it bears naught but weeds, just so is mortification of the desires necessary if the soul is to profit. Without this mortification, I make bold to say, the soul no more achieves progress on the road to perfection and to the knowledge of God of itself, however many efforts it may make, than the seed grows when it is cast upon untilled ground. Wherefore the darkness and rudeness of the soul will not be taken from it until the desires be quenched. For these desires are like cataracts, or like motes in the eye, which obstruct the sight until they be taken away.

St. John of the Cross.
The Interior Castle. First Mansions, Ch. 2

Additional Biblical Reflections: Psalm 6:4, 49:13-20; Isiah 59:10; Matthew 15:14.

Prayer

Lord, we pray that you would do the painful work of weeding our lives of our sins and thereby mortify the garden of our flesh, so the garden of our souls might spring up to the bountiful life you created us to have from the beginning. Grant us the endurance to see through the arduous process of mortification so that we might see the benefits of your bounty. Amen.

DAY 16

We are often like dogs who return to their vomit. Yes, we might make great progress, but how easily do we defile ourselves by returning to old sins that we previously confessed and had purged from our souls. Thus, the saint urges us to take great care about the things we subject our souls to in this world, for all progress can easily be lost when we allow the things that stain and defile our souls to take root.

Meditations from St. John of the Cross

The fourth evil which the desires cause in the soul is that they stain and defile it, as is taught in Ecclesiasticus, in these words: He that toucheth pitch shall be defiled with it. And a man touches pitch when he allows the desire of his will to be satisfied by any creature. Here it is to be noted that the Wise Man compares the creatures to pitch; for there is more difference between excellence of soul and the best of the creatures than there is between pure diamond, or fine gold, and pitch. And just as gold or diamond, if it were heated and placed upon pitch, would become foul and be stained by it, inasmuch as the heat would have cajoled and allured the pitch, even so the soul that is hot with desire for any creature draws forth foulness from it through the heat of its desire and is stained by it. And there is more difference between the soul and other corporeal creatures than between a liquid that is highly clarified and mud that is most foul. Wherefore, even as such a liquid would be defiled if it were mingled with mud, so is the soul defiled that clings to creatures, since by doing this it becomes like to the said creatures. And in the same way that traces of soot would defile a face that is very lovely and perfect, even in this way do disordered desires befoul and defile the soul that has them, the which soul is in itself a most lovely and perfect image of God... It is impossible to explain in words, or to cause to be understood by the understanding, what variety of impurity is caused in the soul by a variety of desires. For, if it could be expressed and understood, it would be a wondrous thing, and one also which would fill us with pity, to see how each desire, in accordance with its quality and degree, be it greater or smaller, leaves in the soul its mark and deposit of impurity and vileness, and how one single disorder of the reason can be the source of innumerable different impurities, some greater, some less, each one after its kind. For, even as the soul of the righteous man has in one single perfection, which is uprightness of soul, innumerable gifts of the greatest richness, and many virtues of the greatest loveliness, each one different and full of grace after its kind according to the multitude and the diversity of the affections of love which it has had in God, even so the unruly soul, according to the variety of the desires which it has for the creatures, has in itself a miserable variety of impurities and meannesses, wherewith it is endowed by the said desires.

St. John of the Cross,
Ascent of Mount Carmel

Additional Biblical Reflections: Ecclesiasticus 13:1; Lamentations 4:7-8; Proverbs 26:11.

Prayer

Dear Lord, there are many ways that we might, by our inattentiveness or passions, defile our souls and find ourselves far from you. Give us the wisdom to see the difference between good things and sinful ones and grant us the resilience to stand up against temptation, so we might rather cherish the intimacy our souls share with you. Amen.

DAY 17

T oday, St. John of the Cross reminds us about the danger of a half-hearted or lukewarm faith. This is one of the many ways in which our desires can plague the soul. With a lukewarm faith, we lack the resolve to stick to any good practice or virtue but are quickly and easily distracted and dissuaded from spiritual pursuits.

Meditations from St. John of the Cross

The fifth way in which the desires harm the soul is by making it lukewarm and weak, so that it has no strength to follow after virtue and to persevere therein. For as the strength of the desire, when it is set upon various aims, is less than if it were set wholly on one thing alone, and as, the more are the aims whereon it is set, the less of it there is for each of them, for this cause philosophers say that virtue in union is stronger than if it be dispersed. Wherefore it is clear that, if the desire of the will be dispersed among other things than virtue, it must be weaker as regards virtue. And thus the soul whose will is set upon various trifles is like water, which, having a place below wherein to empty itself, never rises; and such a soul has no profit. For this cause the patriarch Jacob compared his son Ruben to water poured out, because in a certain sin he had given rein to his desires. And he said: 'Thou art poured out like water; grow thou not.' As though he had said: Since thou art poured out like water as to the desires, thou shalt not grow in virtue. And thus, as hot water, when uncovered, readily loses heat, and as aromatic spices, when they are unwrapped, gradually lose the fragrance and strength of their perfume, even so the soul that is not recollected in one single desire for God loses heat and vigour in its virtue. This was well understood by David, when he said, speaking with God: I will keep my strength for Thee That is, concentrating the strength of my desires upon Thee alone.

St. John of the Cross,
Ascent of Mount Carmel

Additional Biblical Reflections: Genesis 49:4; Psalm 58:10; Luke 12:35-40.

Prayer

Dear Lord, stoke a fire in our souls and a passion for you so that we might be tepid or lukewarm in spiritual matters. Continue to tinder our flames, so we might always grow spiritually and not be easily doused by the storms of life. In Jesus's name. Amen.

DAY 18

In the preceding meditations, St. John of the Cross went after the notion of human desire so poignantly that one might get the idea that it is inappropriate to desire anything at all. In today's meditation, the saint offers helpful clarification about the sorts of desires that are both appropriate and unavoidable as natural creatures and distinguishes these from those that can harm the soul. It is not unholy, for instance, to desire food, clothing, or shelter. However, such desires must be coupled with a pursuit of God. It is not unholy that we should desire our children's safety or other such natural things. These are holy desires, and we must take care not to forsake holy desires as we seek to suppress unholy ones.

Meditations from St. John of the Cross

I expect that for a long time the reader has been wishing to ask whether it be necessary, in order to attain to this high estate of perfection, to undergo first of all total mortification in all the desires, great and small, or if it will suffice to mortify some of them and to leave others, those at least which seem of little moment. For it appears to be a severe and most difficult thing for the soul to be able to attain to such purity and detachment that it has no will and affection for anything.

To this I reply: first, that it is true that all the desires are not equally hurtful, nor do they all equally embarrass the soul. I am speaking of those that are voluntary, for the natural desires hinder the soul little, if at all, from attaining to union, when they are not consented to nor pass beyond the first movements (I mean, all those wherein the rational will has had no part, whether at first or afterward); and to take away these — that is, to mortify them wholly in this life — is impossible. And these hinder not the soul in such a way as to prevent its attainment to Divine union, even though they be not, as I say, wholly mortified; for the natural man may well have them, and yet the soul may be quite free from them according to the rational spirit. For it will sometimes come to pass that the soul will be in the full union of the prayer of quiet in the will at the very time when these desires are dwelling in the sensual part of the soul, and yet the higher part, which is in prayer, will have nothing to do with them. But all the other voluntary desires, whether they be of mortal sin, which are the gravest, or of venial sin, which are less grave, or whether they be only of imperfections, which are the least grave of all, must be driven away every one, and the soul must be free from them all, howsoever slight they be, if it is to come to this complete union; and the reason is that the state of this Divine union consists in the soul's total transformation, according to the will, in the will of God, so that, there may be naught in the soul that is contrary to the will of God, but that, in all and through all, its movement may be that of the will of God alone.

St. John of the Cross,
Ascent of Mount Carmel

Additional Biblical Reflections: Psalm 37:4, 145:19; Luke 6:21; Colossians 3:1-25.

Prayer

Lord, refine our desires so that we might seek only good things in this world, for you created us as creatures in communion with the earth and one another. Thus, let us still seek the good things of this life that you have intended for us, but let us never attach our passions to such things in a way that the creation—rather than you, our creator—becomes God. In Jesus's name. Amen.

DAY 19

We have all prayed, many times, "Thy will be done." Today, St. John of the Cross reminds us about the difference between "thine" and "mine." While we see our will to be conformed to God's, often we find what we desire and what God wills are two different things. However, through spiritual progress, we come to see that our will gradually begins to mirror God's. Yet we can still, even in a state of relative piety, believe that it is thereby safe to pursue our will, for the flesh is always eager to pervert our will. Thus, it is in God's heart that we should always seek His will and check our will accordingly.

Meditations from St. John of the Cross

It is for this reason that we say of this state that it is the making of two wills into one — namely, into the will of God, which will of God is likewise the will of the soul. For if this soul desired any imperfection that God wills not, there would not be made one will of God, since the soul would have a will for that which God has not. It is clear, then, that for the soul to come to unite itself perfectly with God through love and will, it must first be free from all desire of the will, howsoever slight. That is, that it must not intentionally and knowingly consent with the will to imperfections, and it must have power and liberty to be able not so to consent intentionally. I say knowingly, because, unintentionally and unknowingly, or without having the power to do otherwise, it may well fall into imperfections and venial sins, and into the natural desires whereof we have spoken; for of such sins as these which are not voluntary and surreptitious it is written that the just man shall fall seven times in the day and shall rise up again. But of the voluntary desires, which, though they be for very small things, are, as I have said, intentional venial sins, any one that is not conquered suffices to impede union.[4] I mean, if this habit be not mortified; for sometimes certain acts of different desires have not as much power when the habits are mortified. Still, the soul will attain to the stage of not having even these, for they likewise proceed from a habit of imperfection. But some habits of voluntary imperfections, which are never completely conquered, prevent not only the attainment of Divine union, but also progress in perfection.

St. John of the Cross,
Ascent of Mount Carmel

Additional Biblical Reflections: Matthew 6:9-13; Ephesians 1:11; 1 John 2:17.

Prayer

Dearest Lord, might your will be done on Earth as it is in Heaven, not only in our lives but throughout the world. Let our will always be subjected to yours, even as our will comes to reflect yours more consistently. Grant this so that we might progress toward righteousness rather than carnality and constantly grow to be a better reflection of your love and mercy in the world. In Jesus's name. Amen.

DAY 20

It is interesting that St. John of the Cross speaks of faith as the second part of the "dark night" of the soul, which is striving toward God. Nonetheless, faith is truly tested in darkness. When there is light, and all is seen and clear, having faith is easy. When we must traverse through the darkness, unsure about what is in front of us, we must trust the guiding voice of God, who promises to navigate us through this dark night.

Meditations from St. John of the Cross

We now go on to treat of the second part of this night, which is faith; this is the wondrous means which, as we said, leads to the goal, which is God, Who, as we said,] is also to the soul, naturally, the third cause or part of this night. For faith, which is the means, is compared with midnight. And thus we may say that it is darker for the soul either than the first part or, in a way, than the third; for the first part, which is that of sense, is compared to the beginning of night, or the time when sensible objects can no longer be seen, and thus it is not so far removed from light as is midnight. The third part, which is the period preceding the dawn, is quite close to the light of day, and it, too, therefore, is not so dark as midnight; for it is now close to the enlightenment and illumination of the light of day, which is compared with God. For, although it is true, if we speak after a natural manner, that God is as dark a night to the soul as is faith, still, when these three parts

43

of the night are over, which are naturally night to the soul, God begins to illumine the soul by supernatural means with the ray of His Divine light; which is the beginning of the perfect union that follows, when the third night is past, and it can thus be said to be less dark.

It is likewise darker than the first night, for this belongs to the lower part of man, which is the sensual part, and, consequently, the more exterior; and this second part, which is of faith, belongs to the higher part of man, which is the rational part, and, in consequence, more interior and more obscure, since it deprives it of the light of reason, or, to speak more clearly, blinds it; and thus it is aptly compared to midnight, which is the depth of night and the darkest part thereof.

We have now to prove how this second part, which is faith, is night to the spirit, even as the first part is night to sense. And we shall then also describe the things that are contrary to it, and how the soul must prepare itself actively to enter it. For, concerning the passive part, which is that which God works in it, when He brings it into that night, we shall speak in its place, which I intend shall be the third book.

St. John of the Cross,
Ascent of Mount Carmel

Additional Biblical Reflections: Proverbs 3:5-6; Matthew 21:21-22; Hebrews 11:6.

Prayer

Lord, faith is a great gift that you have given us, whereby we must trust your call and heed your voice while navigating periods of darkness. When we need help through our unbelief so that we might persist, see us through the darkness into your light. Amen.

DAY 21

Faith is how we encounter the mysteries of God. When confronted with such mysteries, the rational mind seeks to comprehend God's transcendence, but faith simply accepts it and adores the mysteries, for the goodness of God's mysteries is not contingent on our understanding but His generosity. When we pass through this dark period of the soul, St. John of the Cross reminds us to find ourselves content to adore rather than investigate God's mysteries.

Meditations from St. John of the Cross

Faith, say the theologians, is a habit of the soul, certain and obscure. And the reason for its being an obscure habit is that it makes us believe truths revealed by God Himself, which transcend all natural light, and exceed all human understanding, beyond all proportion. Hence it follows that, for the soul, this excessive light of faith which is given to it is thick darkness, for it overwhelms greater things and does away with small things, even as the light of the sun overwhelms all other lights whatsoever, so that when it shines and disables our visual faculty they appear not to be lights at all. So that it blinds it and deprives it of the sight that has been given to it, inasmuch as its light is great beyond all proportion and transcends the faculty of vision. Even so the light of faith, by its excessive greatness, oppresses and disables that of the understanding; for the latter, of its own power, extends only to natural knowledge, although it has a faculty for the supernatural, whenever Our Lord is pleased to give it supernatural activity.

Even so is faith with respect to the soul; it tells us of things which we have never seen or understood, nor have we seen or understood aught that resembles them, since there is naught that resembles them at all. And thus, we have no light of natural knowledge concerning them, since that which we are told of them bears no relation to any sense of ours; we know it by the ear alone, believing that which we are taught, bringing our natural light into subjection and treating it as if it were not. For, as Saint Paul says, Fides ex auditu. As though he were to say: Faith is not knowledge which enters by any of the senses but is only the consent given by the soul to that which enters through the ear.

St. John of the Cross,
Ascent of Mount Carmel

Additional Biblical Reflections: Matthew 17:20; Luke 17:5; Romans 10:17.

Prayer

Lord, your majesty is far beyond our comprehension. Yet, we are so bold as to presume that we can master our spirituality and, likewise, your Divinity. Grant us humility so that, through faith, we might come to adore your mysteries rather than attempt to subject them to our haughty intellects. Amen.

DAY 22

The irony and wonder of faith is that while it does not grant us complete comprehension of the things of God, it does grant us *understanding*. In today's meditation, we learn that there is a difference between these different sorts of knowledge, for our pursuit of information and knowledge often leads us only deeper into darkness but, with faith, is accompanied by God's revelation, and we find we are illuminated in His truth.

Meditations from St. John of the Cross

And faith far transcends even that which is indicated by the examples given above. For not only does it give no information and knowledge, but, as we have said, it deprives us of all other information and knowledge, and blinds us to them, so that they cannot judge it well. For other knowledge can be acquired by the light of the understanding; but the knowledge that is of faith is acquired without the illumination of the understanding, which is rejected for faith; and in its own light, if that light be not darkened, it is lost. Wherefore Isaias said: If ye believe not, ye shall not understand. It is clear, then, that faith is dark night for the soul, and it is in this way that it gives it light; and the more the soul is darkened, the greater is the light that comes to it. For it is by blinding that it gives light, according to this saying of Isaias. For if ye believe not, ye shall not (he says) have light. And thus faith was foreshadowed by that cloud which divided the children of Israel and the Egyptians when the former were about to enter the Red Sea, whereof Scripture says: *that cloud was full of darkness and gave light to the night.*

A wondrous thing it is that, though it was dark, it should give light to the night. This was said to show that faith, which is a black and dark cloud to the soul (and likewise is night, since in the presence of faith the soul is deprived of its natural light and is blinded), can with its darkness give light and illumination to the darkness of the soul, for it was fitting that the disciples should thus be like the master. For man, who is in darkness, could not fittingly be enlightened save by other darkness, even as David teaches us, saying: *Day unto day uttereth and aboundeth in speech, and night unto night showeth knowledge.* Which, to speak more clearly, signifies: The day, which is God in bliss, where it is day to the blessed angels and souls who are now day, communicates and reveals to them the Word, which is His Son, that they may know Him and enjoy Him. And the night, which is faith in the Church Militant, where it is still night, shows knowledge is night to the Church, and consequently to every soul, which knowledge is night to it, since it is without clear beatific wisdom; and, in the presence of faith, it is blind as to its natural light.

So that which is to be inferred from this that faith, because it is dark night, gives light to the soul, which is in darkness, that there may come to be fulfilled that which David likewise says to this purpose, in these works: *the night will be illumination in my delights.* Which is as much as to say: In the delights of my pure contemplation and union with God, the night of faith shall be my guide. Wherein he gives it clearly to be understood that the soul must be in darkness in order to have light for this road.

St. John of the Cross,
Ascent of Mount Carmel

Additional Biblical Reflections: Exodus 14:20; Isaiah 7:9; Psalm 18:3.

Prayer

Lord, only in faith and trust do we find true understanding. Let us be content with whatever knowledge we might have, not that we might become conceited in our study of your word, but that through it, you might illuminate us in your Spirit. Amen.

DAY 23

Working through St. John of the Cross and his meditations can be a dark night in its own right. As you have undoubtedly experienced, he spends much effort expounding on the darkness or the night of the soul. But this he does for a reason—for even the slightest light shines more brightly in a dark room than one merely dim or already lit. Today, we get a bit of that light to draw us out of the darkness as he explores the benefits we receive when passing through the dark night in faith.

Meditations from St. John of the Cross

Wherefore, passing beyond all that can be known and understood, both spiritually and naturally, the soul will desire with all desire to come to that which in this life cannot be known, neither can enter into its heart. And, leaving behind all that it experiences and feels, both temporally and spiritually, and all that it is able to experience and feel in this life, it will desire with all desire to come to that which surpasses all feeling and experience. And, in order to be free and void to that end, it must in no wise lay hold upon that which it receives, either spiritually or sensually, within itself (as we shall explain presently, when we treat this in detail), considering it all to be of much less account. For the more emphasis the soul lays upon what it understands, experiences and imagines, and the more it esteems this, whether it be spiritual or no, the more it loses of the supreme good, and the more it is hindered from attaining thereto. And the less it thinks of what it may have, however much this be, in comparison with the highest good, the more it dwells upon that good and esteems it, and, consequently, the more nearly it approaches it. And in this wise the soul approaches a great way towards union, in darkness, by means of faith, which is likewise dark, and in this wise faith wondrously illumines it. It is certain that, if the soul should desire to see, it would be in darkness much more quickly, with respect to God, than would one who opens his eyes to look upon the great brightness of the sun.

Wherefore, by blinding itself in its faculties upon this road, the soul will see the light, even as the Saviour says in the Gospel, in this wise: I am come into this world for judgment; that they which see not may see, and that they which see may become blind. This, as it will be supposed, is to be understood of this spiritual road, where the soul that is in darkness, and is blinded as regards all its natural and proper lights, will see supernaturally; and the soul that would depend upon any light of its own will become the blinder and will halt upon the road to union.

St. John of the Cross.
Ascent of Mount Carmel

Additional Biblical Reflections: Proverbs 2:2-5; John 9:39; 2 Timothy 2:7.

Prayer
Lord, too often, we fail to see your light because we have attempted to illuminate our lives artificially. However, your true light can shine more brightly than ever when we pass through the dark nights in faith. Grant us such perseverance. Amen.

DAY 24

Today, St. John of the Cross gives us another metaphor to understand God's work in our souls as He leads us from darkness into light. He compares the process to light striking a window—if the light illumines a room to its greatest capacity, the window must be clean, not stained, fogged, or covered in dust. Today's meditation will help us appreciate the work that God is doing in us as we undergo the process of spiritual refinement.

Meditations from St. John of the Cross

In order that both these things may be the better understood, let us make a comparison. A ray of sunlight is striking a window. If the window is in any way stained or misty, the sun's ray will be unable to illumine it and transform it into its own light, totally, as it would if it were clean of all these things, and pure; but it will illumine it to a lesser degree, in proportion as it is less free from those mists and stains; and will do so to a greater degree, in proportion as it is cleaner from them, and this will not be because of the sun's ray, but because of itself; so much so that, if it be wholly pure and clean, the ray of sunlight will transform it and illumine it in such wise that it will itself seem to be a ray and will give the same light as the ray. Although in reality the window has a nature distinct from that of the ray itself, however much it may resemble it, yet we may say that that window is a ray of the sun or is light by participation. And the soul is like this window, whereupon is ever beating (or, to express it better, wherein is ever dwelling) this Divine light of the Being of God according to nature, which we have described.

In thus allowing God to work in it, the soul (having rid itself of every mist and stain of the creatures, which consists in having its will perfectly united with that of God, for to love is to labour to detach and strip itself for God's sake of all that is not God) is at once illumined and transformed in God, and God communicates to it His supernatural Being, in such wise that it appears to be God Himself, and has all that God Himself has. And this union comes to pass when God grants the soul this supernatural favour, that all the things of God and the soul are one in participant transformation; and the soul seems to be God rather than a soul, and is indeed God by participation; although it is true that its natural being, though thus transformed, is as distinct from the Being of God as it was before, even as the window has likewise a nature distinct from that of the ray, though the ray gives it brightness.

This makes it clearer that the preparation of the soul for this union, as we said, is not that it should understand or perceive or feel or imagine anything, concerning either God or aught else, but that it should have purity and love — that is, perfect resignation and detachment from everything for God's sake alone; and, as there can be no perfect transformation if there be not perfect purity, and as the enlightenment, illumination and union of the soul with God will be according to the proportion of its purity, in greater or in less degree; yet the soul will not be perfect, as I say, if it be not wholly and perfectly bright and clean.

St. John of the Cross,
Ascent of Mount Carmel

Additional Biblical Reflections: Matthew 13:13-16; John 1:13; 1 John 2:11.

Prayer

Lord, cleanse our sin-stained hearts so that your light might illumine our souls more perfectly. We pray that you would help us endure your refinement for the sake of knowing you more intimately, for spiritual progress does not happen when we allow our lives to be clouded by distractions, the things of this world, and sin. In Jesus's name. Amen.

DAY 25

The second "faculty" of the soul which St. John of the Cross says must be refined, after faith, is memory. Memory is a powerful thing. The Israelites were told, for instance, to place a letter on their brows to call the Lord's works to mind. Throughout the Old Testament, how often do we hear God's people reminded about what God did when He rescued Israel from Egypt? So, too, the Passover and other rituals were meant to codify God's actions, in memory, in the hearts and minds of God's people. However, selectively, we often remember only the things that justify our resentments, or we use them to explain our past sins. The memory must be refined like the rest of us so that we aim to increase our recollection of God's good things.

Meditations from St. John of the Cross

The first faculty of the soul, which is the understanding, has now been instructed, through all its apprehensions, in the first theological virtue, which is faith, to the end that, according to this faculty, the soul may be united with God by means of the purity of faith. It now remains to do likewise with respect to the other two faculties of the soul, which are memory and will, and to purify them likewise with respect to their apprehensions, to the end that, according to these two faculties also, the soul may come to union with God in perfect hope and charity... Beginning, then, with natural knowledge, I say that natural knowledge in the memory consists of all the kinds of knowledge

*that the memory can form concerning the objects of the five bodily senses —
namely: hearing, sight, smell, taste and touch — and all kinds of knowledge
of this type which it is possible to form and fashion. Of all these forms and
kinds of knowledge the soul must strip and void itself, and it must strive to lose
the imaginary apprehension of them, so that there may be left in it no kind of
impression of knowledge, nor trace of aught soever, but rather the soul must
remain barren and bare, as if these forms had never passed through it, and
in total oblivion and suspension. And this cannot happen unless the memory
be annihilated as to all its forms, if it is to be united with God. For it cannot
happen save by total separation from all forms which are not God; for God
comes beneath no definite form or kind of knowledge whatsoever, as we have
said in treating of the night of the understanding. And since, as Christ says, no
man can serve two masters,[1] the memory cannot be united both with God
and with forms and distinct kinds of knowledge and, as God has no form
or image that can be comprehended by the memory, it follows that, when
the memory is united with God (as is seen, too, every day by experience), it
remains without form and without figure, its imagination being lost and
itself being absorbed in a supreme good, and in a great oblivion, remembering
nothing. For that Divine union voids its fancy and sweeps it clean of all forms
and kinds of knowledge and raises it to the supernatural.*

St. John of the Cross,
Ascent of Mount Carmel

Additional Biblical Reflections: Exodus 12:14; Luke 22:19-20; John
14:26.

Prayer

Lord, recall to our minds the good deeds you have done so that we might
ever remember your love and faithfulness through these recollections.
Let the memories of our failings serve not as self-justifications but as
causes to rebuff the temptations of the flesh, and may the memories of
your grace, most especially the sacrifice of your Son, be front and center
in our minds. Amen.

DAY 26

After considering the refinement of both faith and memory, St. John of the Cross speaks of the will's conversion. Without the refinement of the will, all of our faculties will be bent awry. To pursue godliness, we must first desire it. This is another purpose of the dark night of the soul—for having gone through such a time, our desire and craving for God's light should grow all the more.

Meditations from St. John of the Cross

We should have accomplished nothing by the purgation of the understanding in order to ground it in the virtue of faith, and by the purgation of the memory in order to ground it in hope, if we purged not the will also according to the third virtue, which is charity, whereby the works that are done in faith live and have great merit, and without it are of no worth. For, as Saint James says: 'Without works of charity, faith is dead.' And, now that we have to treat of the active detachment and night of this faculty, in order to form it and make it perfect in this virtue of the charity of God, I find no more fitting authority than that which is written in the sixth chapter of Deuteronomy, where Moses says: 'Thou shalt love the Lord thy God with thy whole heart and with thy whole soul and with thy whole strength.' Herein is contained all that the spiritual man ought to do, and all that I have here to teach him, so that he may truly attain to God, through union of the will, by means of charity. For herein man is commanded to employ all the faculties and desires and operations and affections of his soul in God, so that all the ability and strength of his soul may serve for no more than this... The strength of the soul consists in its faculties, passions and desires, all of which are governed by the will. Now when these faculties, passions and desires are directed by the will toward God, and turned away from all that is not God, then the strength of the soul is kept for God, and thus the soul is able to love God with all its strength. And, to the end that the soul may do this, we shall here treat of the purgation from the will of all its unruly affections, whence arise unruly operations, affections and desires, and whence also arises its failure to keep all its strength for God. These affections and passions are four, namely: Joy, hope, grief and fear. These passions, when they are controlled by reason according to the way of God, so that the soul rejoices only in that which is purely the honour and glory of God, and hopes for naught else, neither grieves save for things that concern this, neither fears aught save God alone, it is clear that the strength and ability of the soul are being directed toward God and kept for Him. For, the more the soul rejoices in any other thing than God, the less completely will it centre its rejoicing in God; and the more it hopes in aught else, the less will it hope in God; and so with the other passions.

St. John of the Cross,
Ascent of Mount Carmel

Additional Biblical Reflections: Deuteronomy 6:5; Psalm 58:10; James 2:20.

Prayer

Lord, while we desire to know you more, our will is often weak, vacillating between our desires of this world and our desire to embrace your path. Grant us not only access to your holiness but a fervent desire for it. In Jesus's name. Amen.

DAY 27

Our meditations from St. John of the Cross now turn to his *Spiritual Canticle*, consisting largely of songs sung between the bride (the Church) and the bridegroom (Christ). Here we learn more of the intimacy that God intends for those who have passed through the dark night of the soul and what enjoyment there might be for those who come to experience His illumination.

Meditations from St. John of the Cross

The chief object of the soul in these words is not to ask only for that affective and sensible devotion, wherein there is no certainty or evidence of the possession of the Bridegroom in this life; but principally for that clear presence and vision of His Essence, of which it longs to be assured and satisfied in the next. This, too, was the object of the bride who, in the divine song desiring to be united to the Divinity of the Bridegroom Word, prayed to the Father, saying, "Show me where You feed, where You lie in the midday." For to ask to be shown the place where He fed was to ask to be shown the Essence of the Divine Word, the Son; because the Father feeds nowhere else but in His only begotten Son, Who is the glory of the Father. In asking to be shown the place where He lies in the midday, was to ask for the same thing, because the Son is the sole delight of the Father, Who lies in no other place, and is comprehended by no other thing, but in and by His beloved Son, in Whom He reposes wholly, communicating to Him His whole Essence, in the "midday," which is eternity, where the Father is ever begetting and the Son ever begotten.

St. John of the Cross,
The Spiritual Canticle

Additional Biblical Reflections: Song of Solomon 1:6; John 14:3; Revelation 22:17.

Prayer
Dear Lord, to know you is to be members of your Bride united one-in-flesh to the Bridegroom, who is Christ. Let us always keep your Son at the center of our hearts so that we might be conformed to His image in suffering as we pass through the dark night and in resurrection as we embrace the light of His life. Amen.

DAY 28

Today, we reflect on all the progress we have made in the first twenty-seven days, wherein we considered St. John of the Cross's program toward spiritual progress. We are reminded about the things that distress the soul, the theological virtues, and the aspects of the human soul upon which the Lord works to draw us unto Him. All these things work for our good—for the Lord knows better what we require than we know for ourselves.

Meditations from St. John of the Cross

Here the soul speaks of three things that distress it: namely, languor, suffering, and death; for the soul that truly loves God with a love in some degree perfect, suffers in three ways in His absence, in its three powers ordinarily — the understanding, the will, and the memory. In the understanding it languishes because it does not see God, Who is the salvation of it, as the Psalmist says: "I am your salvation."

These three things which distress the soul are grounded on the three theological virtues — faith, charity, and hope, which relate, in the order here assigned them, to the three faculties of the soul — understanding, will, and memory. Observe here that the soul does no more than represent its miseries and pain to the Beloved: for he who loves wisely does not care to ask for that which he wants and desires, being satisfied with hinting at his necessities, so that the beloved one may do what shall to him seem good.

Thus the Blessed Virgin at the marriage feast of Cana asked not directly for wine, but only said to her Beloved Son, "They have no wine." The sisters of Lazarus sent to Him, not to ask Him to heal their brother, but only to say that he whom He loved was sick: "Lord, behold, he whom You love is sick."

There are three reasons for this. Our Lord knows what is expedient for us better than we do ourselves. Secondly, the Beloved is more compassionate towards us when He sees our necessities and our resignation. Thirdly, we are more secured against self-love and self-seeking when we represent our necessity, than when we ask for that which we think we need. It is in this way that the soul represents its three necessities; as if it said: "Tell my Beloved, that as I languish, and as He only is my salvation, to save me; that as I am suffering, and as He only is my joy, to give me joy; that as I am dying, and as He only is my life, to give me life."

St. John of the Cross,
The Spiritual Canticle

Additional Biblical Reflections: Psalm 34:3; John 2:3; John 11:3.

Prayer

Lord, the path of spiritual progress has been laid out in our word and expounded upon by the faithful saint. Grant us the desire to see it through and the perseverance to endure the promises that await us who seek you. Amen.

DAY 29

Spiritual progress is chiefly the work of the Spirit in our hearts. However, if we take such a truth and imagine that we can remain idle and expect God to work on us in our sloth, we are mistaken. Today, St. John of the Cross reminds us that God has made us creatures capable of working, pursuing His word, and striving toward His promised illuminations of the soul.

Meditations from St. John of the Cross

Here the soul makes it known that to find God it is not enough to pray with the heart and the tongue, or to have recourse to the help of others; we must also work ourselves, according to our power. God values one effort of our own more than many of others on our behalf; the soul, therefore, remembering the saying of the Beloved, "Seek and you shall find," is resolved on going forth, as I said just now, to seek Him actively, and not rest till it finds Him, as many do who will not that God should cost them anything but words, and even those carelessly uttered, and for His sake will do nothing that will cost them anything. Some, too, will not leave for His sake a place which is to their taste and liking, expecting to receive all the sweetness of God in their mouth and in their heart without moving a step, without mortifying themselves by the abandonment of a single pleasure or useless comfort.

But until they go forth out of themselves to seek Him, however loudly they may cry they will not find Him; for the bride in the Canticle sought Him in this way, but she found Him not until she went out to seek Him: "In my little bed in the nights I have sought Him Whom my soul loves: I have sought Him and have not found Him. I will rise and will go about the city: by the streets and highways I will seek Him Whom my soul loves." She afterwards adds that when she had endured certain trials she "found Him."

He, therefore, who seeks God, consulting his own ease and comfort, seeks Him by night, and therefore finds Him not. But he who seeks Him in the practice of virtue and of good works, casting aside the comforts of his own bed, seeks Him by day; such a one shall find Him, for that which is not seen by night is visible by day. The Bridegroom Himself teaches us this, saying, "Wisdom is clear and never fades away, and is easily seen of them that love her, and is found of them that seek her. She prevents them that covet her, that she first may show herself to them. He that awakes early to seek her shall not labor; for he shall find her sitting at his doors." [62] The soul that will go out of the house of its own will, and abandon the bed of its own satisfaction, will find the divine Wisdom, the Son of God, the Bridegroom waiting at the door without, and so the soul says: "I will go over mountains and strands."

St. John of the Cross,
The Spiritual Canticle

Additional Biblical Reflections: Song of Solomon 2:1-4; Wisdom 6:13; Luke 11:9.

Prayer

Lord, we too often ask for your spiritual blessings from a posture of idleness, unwilling to do all that is in us to strive toward your graces. Certainly, grace comes by your merits, but we pray you would vivify our efforts so that you might use every step we take to draw us closer to you. In Jesus's name. Amen.

DAY 30

Everything we have learned during our thirty days of prayer with St. John of the Cross—if it were to be comprehended in a single truth—has been focused on the person of Jesus Christ, the Son of God. For He passed through a dark night so that we who follow Him, taking up our crosses in pursuit of Him, might also go with Him through the darkness and be restored alongside Him in the glory of His resurrected life.

Meditations from St. John of the Cross

The son of God is, in the words of St. Paul, "the brightness of His glory and the figure of His substance." God saw all things only in the face of His Son. This was to give them their natural being, bestowing upon them many graces and natural gifts, making them perfect, as it is written in the book of Genesis: "God saw all the things that He had made: and they were very good." To see all things very good was to make them very good in the Word, His Son. He not only gave them their being and their natural graces when He beheld them, but He also clothed them with beauty in the face of His Son, communicating to them a supernatural being when He made man, and exalted him to the beauty of God, and, by consequence, all creatures in him, because He united Himself to the nature of them all in man. For this cause the Son of God Himself said, "And I, if I be lifted up from the earth will draw all things to Myself." And thus in this exaltation of the incarnation of His Son, and the glory of His resurrection according to the flesh, the Father not only made all things beautiful in part, but also, we may well say, clothed them wholly with beauty and dignity.

But beyond all this — speaking now of contemplation as it affects the soul and makes an impression on it — in the vivid contemplation and knowledge of created things the soul beholds such a multiplicity of graces, powers, and beauty with which God has endowed them, that they seem to it to be clothed with admirable beauty and supernatural virtue derived from the infinite supernatural beauty of the face of God, whose beholding of them clothed the heavens and the earth with beauty and joy; as it is written: "You open Your hand and fill with blessing every living creature." Hence the soul wounded with love of that beauty of the Beloved which it traces in created things, and anxious to behold that beauty which is the source of this visible beauty.

St. John of the Cross,
The Spiritual Canticle

Additional Biblical Reflections: Genesis 1:31; Psalm 144:16; John 12:32.

Prayer

Dear Lord, we have access to you only on account of the merits and person of your Son, Jesus Christ. May our lives every be a reflection of His, bearing our crosses so that we might find Him there and endure alongside Him into resurrected life and the illumination of your Spirit. In His name. Amen

www.ingramcontent.com/pod-product-compliance
Lightning Source LLC
Chambersburg PA
CBHW071635040426
42452CB00009B/1634